Unmothered

A Memoir of Survival, Resilience,
and the Search for Family

TONYA KENT

CONTENTS

ACKNOWLEDGEMENTS

First and foremost, I want to give thanks to God, the source of my strength and the One who has guided me through every chapter of this journey. His love, grace, and faithfulness carried me when I couldn't carry myself, giving me hope even in my darkest moments. I am forever grateful for the peace that surpasses all understanding and the purpose He has placed on my life. To God be all the glory.

To my family—those who stood by me, held me up, and reminded me of my worth—your love has been my anchor. Thank you for being my foundation, my support, and my inspiration. Each of you has taught me resilience and grace in ways words cannot capture. This book is as much yours as it is mine, a testament to the strength we find in each other.

To Passion Publications —thank you for your helping hand in shaping this memoir and bringing clarity to my words and purpose to my story. Thank you for breathing life into my voice and helping me tell my story with honesty and authenticity. Your dedication to this work has made it better than I could have ever imagined.

FOREWORD

I remember meeting the author for the first time. She left an impression on me. As I think back, I'm not too sure I could target one particular thing. It could have been the gleaming smile, amazing energy, contagious laughter, or what appeared to be a heart of gold. With her loving eyes affixed on whoever desired her attention, she made those around her feel excited about living.

Afterwards, God saw fit, for a season, to have us work together touching lives while serving others' concerns. Even up until this very day she continues giving selflessly ensuring hurting lives are heard, the rejected are cared for, and the less fortunate are assisted.

In this, her memoir, she sacrificially gives us a glimpse of her personal and private life experiences. I am reminded from it, of what is possible with God's help. By it, we have even a better understanding of her intentionality and motivation for impacting this generation.

I am so honored to know Tonya. I applaud her efforts, persistence, and faith. Most importantly I thank the Almighty God whom we both serve. I am fully convinced her story will be used by Him as a tool to further assist those seeking hope.

May you experience your own personal transformation as you receive the encouragement and strength made available to you from what is written on these pages.

Benjamin Marshall

DEDICATION

To anyone who has been abandoned, abused,
rejected, and left to pick up the broken pieces:
This book is for you.
May you find strength, healing,
and the courage to reclaim your story.

"The Lord is close to the brokenhearted and saves
those who are crushed in spirit."

— *Psalm 34:18*

"Though my father and mother forsake me, the Lord
will receive me."

— *Psalm 27:10*

"He heals the brokenhearted and binds up their
wounds."

— *Psalm 147:3*

A PRAYER FOR HEALING AND WHOLENESS

Dear Lord,

I lift up each heart that reads these words, especially those who carry the weight of abandonment, pain, and rejection. Surround them with Your unending love, and remind them that they are never alone. Heal their brokenness, Lord, and bind up every wound with Your gentle touch.

Fill them with courage to face each day, resilience to rebuild, and hope that transcends their past. May they find strength in Your promises and peace in Your presence. Restore, renew, and remind them of the beauty You see in them.

In Jesus name, Amen.

DEFINITIONS

"Unmothered" -This word immediately draws attention to the absence of a mother figure in your life. It communicates a sense of loss and a unique perspective on your childhood. It's a word that can make readers curious about your story.

"Memoir" -This word indicates that your book is a personal account of your life experiences. Readers will know that they are delving into your memories, emotions, and personal journey.

"Survival" -It suggests that your childhood was marked by challenges and adversity. You've overcome difficult circumstances, and this part of your story is a testament to your strength and resilience.

"Resilience" -This word underscores your ability to bounce back from hardships. It implies that you didn't just survive; you thrived despite the odds. Your resilience is a central theme in your memoir.

"Search for Family" -Your journey involves not only surviving but also seeking a sense of belonging and connection. This part of your story may encompass your efforts to find or build your own "chosen" family.

INTRODUCTION

As the sun dipped below the horizon, casting long shadows over the familiar streets of my childhood, I found myself standing at the crossroads of memory and reflection. In the quiet of that evening, the echoes of my past whispered, beckoning me to unearth fragments of a life that shaped the person I've become.

As we embark on this journey together, my intention is not only to share the fragments of my past but to weave a tapestry of shared humanity. Through the highs and lows, the shadows and light, I invite you to reflect on your own journey. In these pages, we may find common ground, understanding, and perhaps, a shared resilience.

CHAPTER 1

Fragments of Love

In the beginning, there was a void, a hollow space in my young heart where a mother's love should have been. I was three when I was shipped off from the chaos of Los Angeles to the quiet of Berkeley. "Too bad," they said. "Too bad for a mother's love." I didn't understand the words then, but their weight settled into the corners of my soul, shaping my perception of self and family.

My grandmother, a single mother herself, became my lifeline. She wrapped me in her arms and tried to fill the void left by my absent parents. Her love was fierce, but it couldn't erase the ache for a complete family—a longing that echoed in the silent spaces of my childhood.

The neighborhood kids played with their mothers and fathers. I watched, longing for that completeness. I admired a particular family, their unity a balm to my wounded heart. But life, in its cruel twists, led me down a different path, one marred by shadows and pain.

Difficult events unfolded, casting dark clouds over my innocence. I was just a child when the world turned ugly, when the sanctuary of my home was shattered by the hands of strangers. They took more than my innocence; they stole fragments of my soul.

In those moments, I felt utterly alone. The lack of parental love had already chipped away at my self-worth. Now, it shattered what little remained.

Yet, amidst the darkness, glimmers of light seeped through. My grandmother's love, though not a replacement for the missing pieces, became my sanctuary. She taught me resilience, the art of standing tall even when the world tried to break me.

I found solace in the support of others, in friendships that felt like lifelines thrown to a drowning soul. And slowly, painstakingly, I began to rebuild. It was a journey of scars and tears, but also one of unexpected strength.

This memoir is not just a recounting of pain; it's a testament to survival. It's a story of searching for love in the wrong places and, against all odds, finding it within myself. In these pages, I lay bare my wounds, my triumphs, and the enduring spirit that carried me through the darkest nights.

This is my story. This is the story of a girl who dared to survive, to hope, and to heal.

CHAPTER 2

Echoes of Childhood

In this chapter, I step back in time to the echoes of my childhood, a time when the world was still unfolding before me, and my grandmother's love provided a sanctuary amidst uncertainty. She was a mother of six grown children, and I, the youngest, became the apple of her eye.

My earliest memories are painted with the colors of her care. I remember the warmth of her embrace, the tenderness in her voice, and the unwavering love that enveloped me. Despite the physical distance that separated me from my mother, my grandmother filled the void, crafting a nurturing environment that cocooned me.

It was a household with a unique rhythm, with one of my uncles residing with us and the other drifting in and out. My mother and three siblings lived elsewhere, creating a distinct separation that defined our family's dynamics. But within the walls of my grandmother's home, I was spoiled with her love, the kind that only a grandmother could provide.

At a young age, my grandmother placed trust in me, sending me on small errands to the grocery store. I was tasked with a simple list of items, but for some inexplicable reason, I could never make it back without accidentally dropping something needed. The sound of fragile items shattering on the pavement and the sight of groceries strewn about the sidewalk became a common occurrence. I earned the nickname "clumsy" as I made multiple trips to the store to replace what I had broken.

In the realm of childhood, where wants often outweigh the means, my grandmother provided what she could with the modest finances at her disposal. We lived a simple life, devoid of extravagant indulgences, but our bond was solid and unyielding. It was a bond forged through love, resilience, and the unique connection that only a grandmother and her youngest grandchild could share.

As I reminisce about those formative years, I am reminded that childhood is a tapestry of moments, both ordinary and extraordinary. It's a time when love is abundant, and the challenges of the world are met with the unwavering support of a loving guardian.

CHAPTER 3

Yearning for a Mother's Love

There is nothing like yearning for a mother's love. It's a longing that transcends time, distance, and circumstance, a primal need that resides deep within the core of every child. My mother, though not present around the clock, had her moments, and there was a summer when I was twelve that would etch its memory into my heart.

It was during that summer that I learned something new about my family—something that shifted the way I perceived my place in the world. I discovered that I had more siblings, three brothers to be exact. By this age, I hadn't thought much about not being loved by my mother. The prospect of seeing her, reuniting with my sister, and meeting my three brothers overwhelmed me with joy.

My mother was a married woman, yet her role resembled that of a single parent. Her husband was often absent from our home, leaving her to shoulder the immense responsibility of raising her four children on her own. She had it hard; facing a world that often seemed unforgiving. To make ends meet, she worked all types of hours at a betting establishment, where people wagered on horse races. It was a demanding job, and she met its challenges head-on.

But her life was also marred by the weight of her struggles, particularly her heavy consumption of alcohol. It's important to clarify that I don't intend to cast judgment or place blame. My mother was navigating a path filled with obstacles, and she coped with life's challenges as best she could.

The summer when I visited Los Angeles held the promise of reuniting with my family, a short-lived joy that unfolded with unexpected twists. A mysterious illness overcame me, leaving my mother and me perplexed. In search of answers and relief, my mother sent me back to my grandmother's home.

Upon my return, it was my grandmother who recognized what my mother couldn't. She saw that

I was with child, and at the tender age of twelve, I was too young to carry the pregnancy to term. The weight of that decision, the ripple effect it would have on me, was something I would grapple with in the years to come.

This chapter is a journey into the layers of my heart, where the yearning for a mother's love intertwines with the complexities of my family's circumstances, and where the choices we make in the face of adversity can shape our lives in profound ways.

CHAPTER 4

The Sanctuary of Grandma's Home

As I reflect on my upbringing, the memories of Grandma's home emerge as a sanctuary amidst the complexities of my childhood. It's a place where life unfolded in its unfiltered beauty, where I was not just a granddaughter but a part of a tight-knit family.

Growing up wasn't always as pleasant as one might hope. As the youngest child, I never had a room of my own until I reached adulthood and set out on my own journey. I had the unique experience of witnessing the habits of my family, a glimpse into the tapestry of our shared history. The habit of drinking passed down through generations, shaped my early years in ways that left an indelible impact on my life.

From a young age, I saw things that no child should have to witness, and those early impressions carved their mark on my soul. They shaped my upbringing, molding me into the woman I am today. The journey was not without its challenges, but in the midst of those challenges, there were moments of warmth and love that defined my childhood.

The holidays, especially Thanksgiving, were a time of celebration at Grandma's home. She was a master in the kitchen, and the preparations for the big day began a day ahead. She would meticulously craft the menu, preparing the turkey, ham, greens, dressing, and potato salad in advance. This allowed her to focus on the sweet potato pies, cakes, dinner rolls, yams, black-eyed peas, white rice, and warming up the other dishes on Thanksgiving.

One of my fondest memories was sitting at the kitchen table while my grandma prepared two or three different flavored cakes. It was a joyous time, filled with anticipation, as I eagerly awaited the moment when she would hand over the mixing bowls with a little extra batter for me to enjoy. Some might say it wasn't ideal due to the raw eggs, but even in my adult life, I can't resist a lick of cake batter when I'm baking. To me, my grandma was the best cook, a culinary artist hailing from the South.

Grandma's home wasn't a mansion by any stretch of the imagination. It was a modest two-bedroom, one-bath dwelling with a small living room, a compact kitchen, and a tiny laundry area. If I were to estimate, it was no larger than 800 square feet. Yet, within those walls, we created a world of love, connection, and tradition.

During the holidays, the home was a hub of activity. Family members and friends would gather, and there would be conversations flowing in the living room, the kitchen, and even in my uncle's room. People found their own corners to engage in lively discussions, laughter, and shared stories. Our modest home was a place of joy, connection, and celebration.

While my grandmother now resides in heaven, her legacy lives on. My family and I continue the tradition of coming together for the holidays, no matter where life may have taken us. We keep the spirit of togetherness alive, carrying forward the memories and the love that were so abundant in Grandma's home.

CHAPTER 5

A Glimpse of Normalcy

Growing up in the 1960s in Berkeley, California, was a time when community thrived in our neighborhood. It was an era when your next-door neighbor wasn't just a neighbor; they were like family. We knew all the kids' names on the block, and as the years passed, we formed bonds through play and shared school experiences. We became a close-knit group, ready to stand up for one another whenever trouble loomed.

My childhood was marked by a particular family, one that I held in deep admiration. They had about nine children of different ages, which meant there was always laughter and excitement in their home. Two of their daughters were close to my age, my grandmother and their parents shared a profound friendship that was mirrored in our own bond. Over the years, our lives grew together, and even now, at the age of 57, I am still in close contact with my best friend from that family.

We consider each other sisters, and the connection we share is unbreakable. Time and distance may have separated us geographically, but thanks to the wonders of modern technology, our bond remains as strong as ever. Cell phones and Facebook have allowed us to keep in touch and continue the laughter and shared memories from our past.

The family I admired wasn't perfect, despite the presence of two parents in the home. They, too, had their share of challenges, revealing that each family carries its own hidden burdens. The facade of perfection often conceals the turmoil that only surfaces behind closed doors. It's a reminder that the grass isn't always greener on the other side.

As I reflect on my own upbringing, I realize I was blessed to experience both sides of the family dynamic. While I admired the stability of my friend's family, I recognized every family carries its own unique blend of joys and sorrows. We all have our hidden closets filled with secrets and wounds that only time and healing can reveal. These experiences have shaped me, helping me understand there's no one-size-fits-all approach to life and family.

CHAPTER 6

Shadows in the Corner

As I shared in Chapter 4, growing up wasn't always the idyllic experience one might hope for. Despite the sweetness of my grandmother's love, she didn't always make the right choices when it came to relationships with men. She, too, was searching for love in all the wrong places.

For as long as I can remember, the presence of men in her life cast a dark shadow over our home. These men were not just emotionally toxic; they were physically abusive as well. Living under that roof presented a daily challenge, and I witnessed disturbing events that left indelible scars on my young heart.

Nights would be punctuated by yelling, fighting, and the sight of blood splattered on the walls of her bedroom. I would wake up in the middle of the night, my heart pounding with fear. I would fear for my grandmother, and I was traumatized by the scenes I witnessed. Her face, often adorned with black eyes and painful knots, was a sight I couldn't forget.

Every loud conversation made my heart race, and I would tremble, fearing it would escalate into another violent confrontation. Not every argument led to a physical fight, but the threat of violence was always there, a shadow that loomed over our lives.

At times, I longed to escape from that environment, but I couldn't bear the thought of leaving my grandmother behind, vulnerable and alone. The fear of her passing away due to the abuse kept me rooted in that troubled space. My way of seeking solace and escape was to rise early in the morning, between the hours of 5:00 a.m. and 7:00 a.m. I would dress quickly and make my way to my best friend's house, where I'd spend the day in the company of my second family.

The impact of witnessing such behavior at a young age is profound. It left me with emotional scars and challenges that would continue to affect me throughout my life. The shadows in the corner were more than just dark moments; they were the crucible in which I was forged, shaping the person I would become.

CHAPTER 7

Shattered Innocence

In the realm of innocence, there exists a chapter bathed in shadows; a chapter I hesitantly unveil, echoing the silent screams of a child betrayed. It was a summer afternoon, the air thick with the scent of deceit, when my innocence was violently stripped away at a tender age.

How does a young child process such an unfathomable betrayal? The innocence that defined my world was abruptly stolen, leaving a void that echoed with confusion, shame, and terror. The weight of carrying this secret was burdensome, shaping the contours of my existence in ways I couldn't comprehend.

The aftermath of these harrowing experiences left my mind in disarray, sowing confusion about my childhood identity. The wounds etched into my soul manifested in destructive ways. I was only From the tender age of twelve. I stumbled through a path of promiscuity, entering and exiting relationships. A door had opened, leading me into a relentless search for love in the wrong places.

The predator's words, spoken with a chilling threat, warned against revealing the truth. "Don't tell anyone; they won't believe you," he said. Fear became my silent companion. In the aftermath, the silence became a heavy cloak, one I wore to shield myself from the disbelief and judgment I imagined.

After that haunting summer, I never returned. The memory of the violation loomed, a perpetual shadow, a secret destined to accompany me to the grave. Both my grandmother and mother, the anchors of my life, passed with unearthing the truth, that my innocence was robbed not once, but repeatedly by different predators.

CHAPTER 8

A Child's Resilience

In the tapestry of my childhood, woven with threads of hardship and shadows, there emerges a chapter that speaks not of defeat, but of an indomitable spirit—a child's resilience tested by the darkest corners of existence. As I reflect on the tumultuous journey thus far, I uncover the silent strength that propelled me forward.

Amidst the echoes of shattered innocence, my young heart, though bruised, refused to surrender to the weight of despair. It was a resilience forged in the crucible of adversity. How did a child, marked by the scars of violation and abandonment, find the fortitude to endure?

In the absence of a conventional haven, my refuge lay in the fragments of love and stability scattered throughout my tumultuous upbringing. The embrace of a grandmother, flawed yet un-wavering, became a sanctuary. And then there were my friends in the neighborhood. We stuck together through thick and thin. We laughed, played, and somehow made life a bit better for each other.

There was a profound wisdom in the simplicity of childhood, a resilience that arose not from an abundance of resources but from an innate ability to adapt and find joy amidst the chaos. The threads of my resilience were woven from the remnants of shattered innocence, each stitch a testament to the determination of a child refusing to be defined by the darkness that sought to consume.

As I tread through the landscapes of my past, this chapter celebrates the unsung hero within a child resilient, navigating the labyrinth of adversity with an unwavering spirit, finding strength in the unlikeliest of places. It's a testament to the enduring power of the human spirit, even in the face of the most profound challenges.

CHAPTER 9

Bright Spots in the Dark

In the middle of all the chaos, there were these shining moments that kept me going. This chapter is about those lifelines, the things that brought a little light into the darkness.

First off, let's talk about my grandma. Yeah, she had her flaws, but she loved me. Her hugs, her way of making things a bit better; that was my safe place. It might not have been a perfect home, but in her love, I found a kind of warmth that made everything else a bit easier to handle.

And then there were my friends, my partners in crime in the neighborhood. We faced the ups and downs together. Their laughter and the simple joy of playing games with them were like a balm for my soul. When life got too heavy, they were my escape, my refuge.

It's funny how even in the messiest parts of life you can find these little pockets of goodness. Maybe it was a sunny day, maybe a joke that made me laugh till my stomach hurt. Those were the moments I held onto, the rays of light breaking through the dark clouds.

This is a celebration of those moments, the love from my grandma, laughter with my friends, things that kept me going when everything else seemed to want to bring me down. It's about finding light in the middle of the darkest times.

CHAPTER 10

Rising from the Ashes

Life's journey has a way of shaping us, sometimes in ways we never expect. As I grew up, the challenges of my past started to lose their grip, paving the way for a brighter future.

The turning point came when I stepped into Community College. In a social studies class, something remarkable happened. It was there, in a circle of open hearts, that I found the courage to share my story—the story of a twelve-year-old innocence stolen. As those words left my lips, I felt the weight lifting, the darkness unraveling.

To my surprise, my teacher and classmates didn't turn away; instead, they embraced me. Tears flowed, not tears of sorrow, but tears of release. It was as if, in that vulnerable moment, I was cleansed from the pain that had haunted me for years. It felt like a rebirth, a divine intervention washing away the stains of my past.

From that day forward, I carried the torch of my truth into different spaces. The Church became a sanctuary of another kind, teaching me the power of forgiveness. Not just for those who hurt me, but for myself. Letting go of the chains of resentment, I found a newfound freedom; a freedom to define my identity on my terms.

It is a journey rebuilding, healing, and rediscovering self-worth. It's about stepping into the light after years in the shadows, finding hope, resilience, and the strength to forgive; a journey that turned the pain of my past into a source of empowerment.

C L O S I N G   P R A Y E R

"The Lord bless you and keep you; the Lord make his face shine upon you and be gracious to you; the Lord lift up his countenance upon you and give you peace."

Numbers 6:24-26 ESV

ABOUT THE AUTHOR

Tonya Kent is a mother and grandmother who was once like many of the ladies she has the privilege of assisting. For many years, she was stuck in a dreadful cycle of depression, suicidal thoughts, and unhealthy relationships. In her mind, she was in prison. It was not until she committed to a relationship with God that her life began to transform radically.

She has now earned three A.A. degrees in Human Services, Universal Studies: Social Science and Liberal Studies. She also attended UC Davis earning a B.A. degree in Women's Studies.

In addition to being a Pastoral Care Counselor and Author, she currently serves as a chaplain in the LaVista Correctional Facility, Pueblo, CO. This is a result of her passion to help mothers be reunited with their children and gain freedom from mental and emotional turmoil and have a second chance.

Tonya is the Chief Executive Director of Infinite Hope and Restoration Ministries 'Second Chance Mothers' Mentorship' program (IHRM). IHRM is a loving faith-based non-profit 501 (c) (3) reentry organization, dedicated to providing transitional housing (coming soon) and reentry support to mothers with young children who are exiting from County, State, and Federal Correctional Institutions.